WHAT NOW?

JUDGE BILL SWANN

BALBOA.PRESS

A DIVISION OF HAY HOUSE

Balboa Press books may be ordered through booksellers or by contacting:

Balboa Press
A Division of Hay House
1663 Liberty Drive
Bloomington, IN 47403
www.balboapress.com
844-682-1282

Print information available on the last page.

ISBN: 979-8-7652-4426-5 (sc)
ISBN: 979-8-7652-4425-8 (e)

Library of Congress Control Number: 2023914437

Balboa Press rev. date: 08/04/2023

Contents

Dedication

Diana, my love, there are places we've wanted to go. But time and our granddaughter kept us from going to those places.

The places don't matter. We will stroll over heaven together. When this world has vanished away, I will stroll over heaven with you.

You showed me that Bruce Springsteen puts it this way: *If I should fall behind, you wait for me. If you fall behind, I'll wait for you.*

Preface

The possibilities I imagined in *What If?* were merely things to be explored by an unfettered mind. Things that might happen in an imaginary world. Or as my oldest son put it, when we "think outside the box."

Now let's put those things back into the box. Let's look at each of those odd happenings and figure out how it will be when they go away. When the dystopian event becomes normal again.

There are other pieces in this book, and some poetry too. You are going to have fun. Enjoy!

A little good news

The twenty-four hour news cycle gives us garbage. Wall-to-wall and constantly.

In 1983, Canadian Anne Murray had had enough. She struck back with, "A Little Good News." Her song was enthusiastically embraced: a #1 single for twenty weeks.

> *I came home this evening*
> *I bet the news will be the same*
> *Somebody takes a hostage*
> *Somebody steals a plane*
>
> *I want to hear the anchor*
> *Talk about a country fair*
> *And how we cleaned up the air*
> *How everybody learned to care*
> --copyright, ASCAP

We have all had enough bad news, enough garbage,

Also by Judge Bill Swann

The Techniques of Softening: E.T.A. Hoffmann's Presentation of the Fantastic, 1971, Yale University Press

Five Proofs of Christianity, 2016, Westbow Press

Politics, Faith, and Love, 2017, Balboa Press

Kirksey, 2021, Balboa Press

More Kirksey, 2021, Balboa Press

The Judith Files, 2021, Balboa Press

What If?, 2022, Balboa Press

All the above are available from the publishers, from Amazon, and from www.judgebillswann.com.

Acrophobia

"Acro" is a prefix meaning height. Thus, "acrophobia" means fear of heights. I have it. Even ladders bother me. However, I have no problem standing at a window in a tall building and looking down to the ground. I have no problem with hot air ballooning. I did it often.

I have no problem climbing trees. I broke my arm at six years old falling from a pear tree in Covington, Georgia. This was the summer of 1947 or 1948. I can remember the chloroform drips falling onto my face mask as I lay on the hospital table. (Chloroform was used as an anesthetic between the 19th century and the first half of the 20th century. It is horrible.)

As a ninth grader at Webb School in 1956, I climbed the outside of Sequoyah Presbyterian Church. So, no acrophobia at that point.

My paternal grandmother, Stella Upshaw Swann, had such a fear of heights that she had to lie on the floor of the back seat of my parents' car as we drove to Newfound Gap in the Smokies.

According to the Cleveland Clinic, acrophobia is one of the most common phobias. Approximately 3% to 6% of people have acrophobia. There is no agreement as to whether it is a genetic trait or a learned behavior.

Advice

Once upon a time there was a mother with a teenage son, a good boy. But she was worried. She knew all the possible mistakes that lay ahead of him--all the decisions he would have to make--and, being his mother, she knew he would make some of them wrong.

She knew that he would have to make his own errors, that she couldn't shield him forever. She knew that mistakes don't hurt you if you can recover, learn from them.

But she didn't just want to step back and let him guess. She wanted to give him, gently, a little life wisdom. She wanted to keep it simple, hoping he would remember her advice.

So she told him five things: _One_, give your life a gentle pace. _Two_, remember hard times don't last forever. _Three_, love a woman. _Four_, love God. _Five_, put the peace of your soul ahead of money, ahead of accomplishments.

With that, she figured she had said it all.

She knew that after giving her advice she would only be able to repeat it for him now and again, if he should need it.

What do this mother's five points have to do with the misery of the courtroom?

People I saw in litigation knew the five things, or would learn them later in life. But on court day, life's tumult roared on.

A judge sits beside the turnpike of life. A gatekeeper beside the fumes, roaring motors, the money thrown into toll baskets, new directions taken quickly.

The mother's five-point plan is in a 1973 song by Gary Rossington and Ronnie Van Zant. These guys are not from Harvard. They're from Doraville, Georgia. They are the lead vocal and lead/rhythm guitar in the southern rock and roll band called Lynyrd Skynyrd. Interestingly enough, they sang long and hard against whiskey and drugs. Rossington and Van Zant, writing in their twenties, give us a mother who cares about her son:

> *mama told me*
> *when I was young*
> *sit beside me*
> *my only son*
> *and listen closely*
> *to what I say*
> *and if you do this*
> *it'll help you*
> --Copyright BMI

Good things can come in strange packages. Get your kids a digitally remastered Skynyrd CD, call everyone into the family room, and crank it up loud. The guitar will terrify the cat, but your kids will love it. You'll be nominated for Parent Of The Year. And it will be your lead-in to talk about values.

Appearances differ again

In the world I looked at in *What if?* I imagined that there were no recognizable ethnicities. Everyone looked alike. Passport photos were useless.

But in our world of today, photographs are back in our passports.

Racial discrimination thrives.

The United Negro College Fund finds its donations increase each month. The same for the American Civil Liberties Union.

The Democratic party returns happily to its balkanization of the electorate.

Baby birds and squirrels

Lions eat zebras. Squirrels eat baby birds. Some people think this is wrong. My best friend thinks it is wrong.

One afternoon in Northwest Ontario we were playing cards beside a nest of burrowing birds. We had seen an adult bird coming and going in the tunnel. Then a squirrel entered the tunnel, came out with two baby birds, and ate them. Right in front of us. No shame. Then he went back into the tunnel for more.

"Goddamnit! Did you see that?" John said. "If I had my gun I would kill him!"

"John," I said, "it's just the natural thing. Creatures eat each other. We just don't see it very often. Lions kill hyenas. Is that wrong?"

"Damn right it's wrong."

"Get used to it."

Biden is a disaster

Three years of failure. In Afghanistan: surrender of Bagram air force base, precipitous withdrawal, people falling off airplanes, millions of dollars of weapons left behind for the Taliban.

An open border with Mexico, fentanyl coming in from the Mexican cartels, fentanyl made in China and supplied to the cartels by China.

Criminals essentially unprosecuted in Portland and San Francisco. No comment from the White House.

Hunter Biden, his laptop, and his father: "My son has done nothing wrong." "I am proud of him."

Biden's cognitive decline, for which we can have only sympathy.

But there is much worse to come: Biden will resign if he is reelected, in order to give us America's first female president. That is the game plan.

Birches

I had a post-divorce case in which a parent testified, "All I want is to create an island in the chaos, a place where my children can be peaceful, where they will be protected."

It was a case like hundreds of cases. Two children. Two parents. Some good years of marriage, some bad. Then a divorce.

But it was not over on divorce day. Not by a long shot. Divorce was just the overture to a long opera which followed. The litigation had only sounded a few themes and hinted at others. The musicians then paused, drew fresh post-divorce breath, the curtain rose, and the themes from the overture received full elaboration.

The parent who testified, "All I want is to create an island in the chaos," knew what the children needed. An end to the back-and-forth struggle, a quiet place.

> *It's when I'm weary of considerations,*
> *And life is too much like a pathless wood*
> *Where your face burns and tickles with the cobwebs*
> *Broken across it, and one eye is weeping*
> *From a twig's having lashed across it open.*
> *I'd like to get away from earth awhile*
> *And then come back to it and begin over.*
> --Robert Frost, "Birches"

That parent wanted another chance. An opportunity for a fresh and peaceful start, so that he/she could do it right this time.

> *When I see birches bend to left and right*
> *Across the lines of straighter darker trees,*
> *I like to think some boy's been swinging them.*
> *But swinging doesn't bend them down to stay*

As ice-storms do . . .
I should prefer to have some boy bend them
As he went out and in to fetch the cows--
Some boy too far from town to learn baseball,
Whose only play was what he found himself,
Summer or winter, and could play alone.
One by one he subdued his father's trees
By riding them down over and over again . . .
So was I once a swinger of birches.
And so I dream of going back to be.

If that parent who wants a quiet place has a chance, the new beginning will be a calm one. There will be a tolerance of the other parent.

The parents will come to know that their children learn more from *how* they do what they do as parents than from *what* they do as parents.

One of the many blessings of parenting is that new beginnings can be made. The skill for parents lies in recognizing when they are trapped in a pathless wood.

Cambric tea

My mother made a huge cup of light-colored tea for me every school morning, using no sugar and lots of milk. She used a black tea, English Breakfast.

Mother just called it "cambric tea" and I didn't know why it had such a name. After she died, I learned that cambric is a color. It is the color of flax.

Cambric is also a fine dense cloth, a lightweight plain-weave fabric, originally from the commune of Cambrai in northern France.

Claustrophobia

My grandmother Effie did not like small spaces. Even elevators were too tight for her. She told me that she needed to be "really dead" before being put in a coffin. Probably she had heard about people in the cold waters off the Maine coast reviving after having been thought drowned.

My first encounters with claustrophobia were in a cave we went to as Boy Scouts. There was a tight passage about six feet long we had to work through to get to a large room beyond. I did it often, and never liked it. I had no term for the unpleasant feeling. I had never heard of claustrophobia. But that is what it was.

Decades later as an adult I had several MRIs in machines with tubes. They were called "closed" MRI machines. I coped by insisting on earphones with music and something to cover my eyes. Claustrophobia.

Corn pone

My Grandfather Swann (born William Kirksey Swann) made corn pone in Covington, Georgia. My father and I kept it up in Tennessee. It is thin and crunchy.

> white or yellow corn meal (not self-rising)
> ½ tsp. salt
> cold water
> olive oil
> preheated 375-degree oven
> butter (not margarine)

Rinse and dry a cast iron griddle or skillet if it hasn't been used in a while. Scour it with a wad of paper towel, damp with olive oil. Put a small dollop of oil into the skillet or griddle and spread it around covering the entire bottom and sides up about half an inch. (The batter will be so thin it will not climb the sides.)

The skillet or griddle needs to be significantly damp with oil. If there is too much, daub it up with a paper towel.

Put the meal into a medium large bowl. Start with a cup. Add the salt. Turn a cold faucet on slightly, and put the bowl under it for a moment. Mix the batter with one hand.

Add water in dribs until it is a thick soup. The batter must be soupy. Dump it onto the center of the griddle or skillet. Jerk the griddle or skillet left and right to spread the batter. If it doesn't reach the edges, mix another soupy batch and dump it in the middle of the first one. Repeat the jerking.

Make sure the oven is at 375 degrees.

Bake for 20 minutes and check. It probably won't be done. It may need five more; check again. It may need yet another five.

Bake the pone until there is brown at the edges, and maybe at some of the thin spots.

Serve with real butter.

Dystopia, dysphoria, utopia, euphoria

A *dystopia* is a speculated society which is undesirable or frightening. It is often treated as an antonym of utopia, a term coined by Sir Thomas More. *Utopia* is the title of More's best known work. It was published in 1516 presenting a blueprint for an ideal society with minimal crime, violence, and poverty.

Dystopias often have fear, tyrannical governments, environmental disaster, and other things associated with cataclysmic decline. Themes are complete control through propaganda, censoring of information, denial of free thought, worship of an unattainable goal, loss of individuality, and enforcement of conformity.

A *utopia* is an intentional community. Hypothetical utopias focus on equality in economics, government, and justice, with the implementation varying based on ideology.

There are socialist, capitalist, monarchical, democratic, anarchist, ecological, feminist, patriarchal, egalitarian, hierarchical, racist, left-wing, right-wing, reformist, free love, nuclear-family, extended-family, gay, lesbian, and other utopias.

The opposite of a utopia is a dystopia.

Dysphoria is a state of unease or dissatisfaction. It is the semantic opposite of euphoria. In a psychiatric context, dysphoria may accompany depression, anxiety, or agitation.

Intense states of distress and unease increase the risk of suicide. Relieving dysphoria is a priority of psychiatric treatment. Dissatisfaction with being able-bodied can be diagnosed as "body integrity dysphoria."

"Gender dysphoria" is distress due to the primary sex characteristics assigned at birth.

Euphoria is well-being. Aerobic exercise, laughter, music, and dancing can induce euphoria. It can be a symptom of mania. Romantic love and human sexual response can induce euphoria. Addictive drugs can induce euphoria.

East Berlin 1968

World War II ended with Germany divided into four sectors--

American, British, French, and Russian. The capital of the defeated nation, Berlin, was divided into the same four sectors. The three western sectors of the city were rebuilt. Capitalism flourished. War-damaged buildings were repaired. Not so in East Berlin. Bombed-out buildings remained empty. Shoppers could buy only what central planners decided should be available.

So when Mary and I visited East Berlin we took bananas and nylon stockings to our friends. Our friends could buy pigs knuckles in glass jars and bread, but they could not buy washing machines or Western newspapers.

Everyone had a job, and earned a pittance. Their joke was, "We pretend to work and they pretend to pay us." The exception was high officials in the SED--the *Sozialistische Einheitspartei Deutschlands*--who had plenty of money and access to western goods. They had stockings and bananas.

So East Berlin and all the eastern sector of Germany languished in a centrally-planned economy.

It is not just a matter of stockings and bananas. The central planners could have decided to provide those. But the rest of the economy would still have remained under central planning. And it would be clear to all the world that economies defy central planning.

Economies are too complex for planners--no matter how well intentioned. So from the end of the war in 1945 to the fall of the Berlin wall on November 9, 1969, all of East Germany and East Berlin had no bananas or stockings.

East Berlin garden plots

The people of East Berlin lived in tiny, walk-up apartments. The buildings were five stories tall.

But central planners did provide small garden plots outside the city. They were fenced sixteen-foot squares. There the city people could grow the vegetables they could not buy in East Berlin. Many East Berliners slept in their garden plots when work schedules permitted.

The people needed the out-of-doors, freedom from regimentation, a place to look at the sky and say, "I have made my sixteen-foot escape."

Envy

Envy, sweet envy. "If only I had . . . then I would be happy."

There is another option. Thomas Stearns Eliot (1888-1965) puts it like this:

> *Because I do not hope to turn again*
> *Because I do not hope*
> *Because I do not hope to turn*
> *Desiring this man's gift and that man's scope*
> *I no longer strive towards such things*

But it requires dedicated thought to stop striving. Hard distinctions must be made as to which strivings are for vanity and which are proper ambitions.

> *Teach us to care and not to care*
> *Teach us to sit still*

Much of T.S. Eliot's "Ash Wednesday" is a prayer for peace.

When I think of parents and their hard job of parenting, I think about the peace of sitting still. Showing children we can be at rest.

Children will have days in which "all" their friends have Nintendo shoelaces, and they "need some too." These are the days in which parents have to figure out whether the shoelaces are (1) indeed a necessity, (2) a harmless conformity, or (3) a significant issue over which the parents will risk tears.

Fortunately "all my friends" falls into category (2).

But "all my friends are doing drugs, Daddy." Now parents must make things clear. This falls in category (3). Now's the time to talk about values.

Perhaps parents should realize that their own desire for a Rolex watch is the same as the glittering shoelaces.

Perhaps the parents are vexed at having gotten less in life's bazaar. Less than the Joneses. Perhaps they wonder where the Joneses go on vacation, and whether they are keeping up with the Joneses.

Envy is the sixth of the seven deadly sins, and like the other five, it has a two-fold importance: *what the parents* _model_, and *what they* tell *the children.*

A slippery subject matter. It is simply not true that we do not envy.

What is envy? It is just comparison, with a little desire added. It is natural. It is human. It is probably a genetically-wired survival skill.

So what should parents tell their children about envy? After all, the children should have a fair shot at possessions. At material comfort.

As Jane Austen puts it in the opening sentence of *Pride and Prejudice*, regarding Mrs. Bennet (who has two single daughters), "It is a truth universally acknowledged that a single man in possession of a good fortune must be in want of a wife."

So, a balancing act: enough envy, enough capitalism to maintain a protective coloration of self-respect when grouped with peers. But not more than that. Lest we become clotheshorses.

Parents need to tell their children how to distinguish between necessary self esteem and slavery to needs. The parents must speak of family, loyalty, religious faith, ethics, respect for institutions, and friendship. Big, hard topics.

During the Nazi genocide, Jewish parents at their own open mass graves were seen--just before being shot--embracing their children, pointing to heaven, and talking intently to the little ones. None of us will have such a challenge, but we do have the ultimate issues.

Envy is a lesser challenge. It is _where_ we live. But it does not need to be _how_ we live.

Evil

The Germany that produced Luther, Goethe, Schiller, and Bertolt Brecht also produced cattle cars for human transport, gas chambers for entire families, and round-the-clock cremation.

In Washington there is a holocaust museum. I have not been there, but I will go. It is said to be factorylike, prisonlike.

However, I went to Dachau in 1962, Auschwitz in 1971, and in 1991 I went to the camp set in a beech forest known as Buchenwald. Johann Wolfgang von Goethe lived in Weimar next to the Buchenwald. His house is still there. I have visited that house. But uphill from his house is what became the extermination camp Buchenwald.

In the iron entrance gate is a lying promise, "Arbeit macht frei"--"work will set you free."

Part of the way I made *myself* free was to write about it.

Wind scours these pillows,
The arcs for barracks,
Where slept the odd ones,
Needing whipping,
The somewhat different Sabine stones.
Carried screaming, carried weeping,
Up, on shoulders, groped and fondled,
Sweaty shoulders, spittled hands.
Carried here for breaking, grading,
Fluffing, patting, plumping up,
Fluffed up beds for consummation,
Ettersburger Ruhestaette.

We force our hands into our pockets,
Feel for stitches, tick threads there,
Ticking threads now one by one:
Will this ground come clean again?

We know that some stains lack all purge,
That deeds can cry and lack reply,
We know some things will be remembered,
Noted, writ down, not forgot,
Etched in memory, never grasped.

This forest stretches down the hill,
Past Russian barracks, new ones once,
Down the hill, they reach to Weimar,
Town where air is brown and old,
Town where lignite falls on roof tiles,
Town where ash falls back on sills,
Back on roof tiles, Goethe's curtains,
Falls on pillows, lies at peace,
On pillows brown in Weimar town.

Up here, the hill above the town,
The wind is roaring, scrubbing pillows.
It scrubs this suburb no one knew.
Oh, no one, no one, had a clue.
Here stones were lifted,
Laid for pleasure,
Broken, raped, in spite of weeping.

Here the pillows carry numbers,
Gray and white, laid out in order.
Landscape arcs, Teutonic neatness,
No brown ash, no lignite here.
The scouring wind drives grit up here.

The people don't come up from town,
The people don't come up to frown,
Don't come up and shake their heads,
Don't come up to view these beds.
The consummation that was here--
"Ach ja," they say, "we don't go near."

Fainting

When I was a teenager I often made rounds with my surgeon father. Fort Sanders, Baptist, St. Mary's, the old General. All the hospitals. He used back roads to get from one to the next as fast as possible.

I had been in open-heart surgery with him several times, but I had not seen him open a chest. Other surgeons did that, and we would come in only when it was time to do the actual heart surgery.

One day at the old General my father did a spinal tap. The patient was leaning forward. The injection site had been sterilized. Daddy took a large needle and put it in the man's back. I fainted.

I fell quietly against the wall behind me and slid to the floor. In a bit, I woke up with Daddy grinning at me. He was not embarrassed but I was.

Family

Families matter in at least three ways.

<u>First</u>, the family is all that some of us have. For some of us it is our only security, our only continuity with the past, our only hope for happiness further down the road. This is painfully so with the termination of a long marriage. One spouse--sometimes both--faces economic upheaval, sometimes economic disaster, with a divorce. After a long marriage it often happens that one spouse is effectively unemployable outside the home.

<u>Second</u>, for many of us, family is our most important emotional possession. There are many scenarios, but the most recurrent is the loss of traditional family routines. No longer, after the litigation ends, will mother or dad come home to the children seven days a week. Some of those days he or she will come home to an empty house--a crushing change.

<u>Third,</u> and overstating it a bit, the family is the last bastion of traditional values. The family keeps the Mongol hordes at bay. Without the family, Genghis Khan in his many forms--drugs, immorality, a dying work ethic--will sweep in and take us captive.

And for people who care about the family, all three points have validity. The family is our contact with past and future. Touching the past may be painful to us. We may fear what the future will bring to us or to other members of our family. But the family is rootedness in the continuum of time. Like or dislike our family's past, like or dislike its present, the family defines a part of us.

We know ourselves fully only if we understand the family we grew up in. We are better able to help others, more able to serve, when we have a sound sense of who we are.

The family we create--our family of procreation, as opposed to our family of orientation/upbringing--is our chief accomplishment or failure. We will see it and feel it as such.

There is no love, no emotion, no protectiveness more definite than that of a parent for a child. It will not be compromised. It is both voluntary and instinctive. It forms the basis of conscious choices--I will spend this time with my child instead of at the office. And it is the basis of unreflected choices--I will put my body between my child and the rolling car, no matter the consequences to me.

This intense love can go astray if it is entwined with the parent's self-concept. If it is the father and not the mother who has the problem (and it usually is the father), his son must make excellent grades, he must be on the basketball squad's first team.

The demand comes from the father's own inchoate insecurity. He is rooted in his own fear of failure, his fear of exposing his own weakness. He worries that his own incompleteness will be revealed through an incomplete son.

We know that love does not usually go astray. We know the family can teach the values we need. Work ethic. Sobriety.

Insecure parents do not raise secure children--unless and until those parents understand and overcome their own fears.

A simple start for such a parent is to say, "My parenting is suffering because I am uneasy. What is worrying me is . . ." If the source of uneasiness can be admitted, the parent is free to deal with his/her children with thought rather than fearful reflex.

The family can defeat the Mongol hordes--both the ones outside the house and those camped out in the living room.

Fire exists again

In the world of *What if?* I imagined that fire was gone.

That matches would not light. That there were no candles, no gas stoves, no kerosene or gas lanterns.

That no internal combustion engines could work, so there was no transportation, no shipping.

But in our normal world, with fire yielding its usual benefits, we have our engines working again, normal shipping, normal transportation, and we have lights at night.

Five flavors

Smell is in the nose and taste is in the mouth. When I brew tea with my Keurig, I taste the richness of English Breakfast. After I add milk and heat it in the microwave, I savor the richness of the milk.

When I toast raisin bread, I smell it. When I eat it, I taste the raisins and the wheat of the bread.

There are four traditional flavors: sweet, sour, bitter, and salty. To these has been added "umami," a Japanese word for "delicious taste." It is produced by certain amino acids. It has a "savory" flavor, released by cooking, curing, or aging. Umami foods include seared and cured meats, aged cheeses, fish sauce, green tea, soy sauce and cooked tomatoes.

There is speculation that a sixth flavor will soon be recognized: "fatty."

Fraudulent Christmas letters

Fraud is not one of the seven deadly sins. It abounds during the Christmas season. It is being introduced into America by foreign agents in the letters we get.

Albanian communists write these letters, the ones that appear to come from out-of-town friends, telling us how very well their children are doing in school, in sports, and in upwardly-mobileness.

And how one spouse has a rewarding but exhausting job that fulfills him/her but leaves little time for (fill in the blank). And how marvelously the other spouse is coping with the challenges of career while finding time to (fill in the blank) and still enjoy and assist in all the achievements of the children.

They have just moved into a new house, and only recently returned from Hawaii, where one of the parents presented a paper on brain surgery. They make apple bran muffins at home. The recipe is included.

The image in these letters: *We are very busy, very well adjusted, very successful, and you aren't.* They all but tell us Benjamin Spock knows we fail as parents.

It may not be just Albanians who send these letters. Fidel Castro was seen with drafts.

Do not be taken in. It is not your friends who are writing this stuff. Merchants of inferiority want you to feel bad. They pose as your friends and send you the letters. Because if we think we don't measure up to our model parent friends, this will weaken us. Then we can be taken over by the foreign powers. Sort of an Albano-Cuban hegemony. From sea to shining sea, none of us measuring up and all of us ripe for invasion.

The foreign powers know that it's hard to stay married, hard to be a parent. They think they can push us over the edge.

Well, we can do something. We can fight back. Truth is a mighty weapon. We can do surveillance on all the Ralphs and Beckys who send us these letters. We can find the fly-in-the-ointment stuff. Like Ralph Jr. being kicked off the basketball team.

Or we can meet personally with all the Ralphs and Beckys--this will take time--and tell them we don't expect them to be perfect. That they don't have to give us this *"every day in every way growing better and more prosperous"* stuff. Tell them that we know they are frightened about life's dark valleys and so they write this hokum about mountaintops.

These meetings may get a little hostile. Wear loose clothes and keep a roll of nickels in your pocket. Believe me, Ralph and Becky will thank you later.

If you feel you don't have the time for meetings and possible fisticuffs-- even with all the time you save by buying your muffins instead of baking healthy togetherness muffins--there is still something you can do.

Go to a big grocery store where you get your muffins. Buy a tabloid in the checkout line. Clip the story about "Woman Raped in Space Ship by Dog-like Aliens." There's one in every issue. Details vary. Don't worry. It will be close enough.

Make photocopies. This will violate copyright laws, but hey, a nation is at stake. Mail these out as your holiday letter. Year after year. It's OK to put in your own family photos along with the story.

It's not much, but it's a statement. What you're saying is: "If you can believe this tabloid stuff, I can believe your Christmas letters."

Friction returns

In the world of *What if?* I imagined that cars, trains, and trucks had no traction. There was gravity, but no traction.

But with friction restored, vehicles can move again. They have traction.

And there is less reliance on water transportation, which had blossomed when friction was gone.

Greed

Greed is the hunger for more. More things, more possessions, more activities in an already busy day. Some people call it enhancement. The church calls it greed, one of the seven deadly sins.

> *I am riding on a limited express,*
> *one of the crack trains of the nation.*
> *Hurtling across the prairie into blue haze and dark air*
> *go fifteen all-steel coaches holding a thousand people.*
> *(All the coaches shall be scrap and rust*
> *And all the men and women laughing*
> *in the diners and sleepers shall pass to ashes.)*
> *I ask a man in the smoker where he is going*
> *and he answers: "Omaha."*

There are a lot of parents headed for Omaha. They are goal-set parents who cannot hear their children. Who cannot hear the arteries' pulsing song of mortality, of numbered days, of the privilege to live this one day. Because they are deaf, headed to Omaha.

The poem is Carl Sandburg's "Limited."

For many of us, the present moment is not to be savored. We are not at peace. We are preparing to pull down our barns and build larger ones. Because of this, we do not know that all the children want us to do is sit in the playhouse and listen, just listen.

The skill of listening is not taught in school. It is the greatest gift we can give children, after love. Perhaps the act of attending is the chiefest part of love. We leave our agendas. We step outside the hurtling crack train of the nation.

Faust wanted an enhanced life--was willing to trade his soul for it. More knowledge, power, land, sex, youth. Younger women, faster horses, older whiskey. Professor Faust felt safe to wager his soul on the bet that he would never have a moment in which he would be so content that he would wish it to last forever.

The early Mick Jagger was greedy, but then he realized

> *You can't always get what you want.*
> *No, you can't always get what you want.*
> *But if you try sometime*
> *You might just find*
> *You get what you need.*
> --Abkco Music and Records

When Scrooge woke on Christmas morning he was joyous at his opportunity to live that one day. That joy stayed with him each and every day thereafter. And Tiny Tim did not die. Scrooge became the benefactor of the Cratchit family, gave Bob plenty of coal for the office fire, and made Tiny Tim his special favorite.

When we read "A Christmas Carol", we see that each day is an opportunity. The problem lies in remembering it. The problem is staying out of Omaha.

Grits, revisited

I have written before about this, my favorite food.

>one teaspoon of salt
>one quart of water
>butter, not margarine
>one cup old fashioned, stone ground, slow cooking grits
>(never "five minute," or "quick cooking" grits)
>grated cheese or sour cream (optional)
>black pepper

Bring the water and salt to a boil. Grits will stick, so put some butter into the boiling water before you whisk in the grits. Turn the heat to low, and put a lid on the pot.

Don't touch anything for twenty minutes, then check the consistency. If it is too wet, keep cooking. When it is done, you can whisk in cheese or sour cream. If not that, whisk in some butter.

Pour it all into a bowl, dot it with butter, and serve with freshly ground black pepper.

At the Chocolate Moose in International Falls, a fine place for breakfast, there are no grits. And never will be, according to the waitress. When we order them, she says "No!" We then say "Please." She says "No!" again. She thinks that grits have to do with moral imperfection.

Gun violence

It just keeps happening week after week, sometimes day after day. Shooters kill innocent people. Shooters target and kill cops.

All decent people want it to end. One solution is to remove all the guns from America. It is frequently proposed.

The Second Amendment guarantees Americans the right to keep and bear arms. Let us imagine that the Second Amendment gets repealed. There is a process in the Constitution for doing that. We repealed Prohibition. Imagine that the Second Amendment has been repealed. Then the time comes to remove the guns.

Now comes the time to trust that it can be done. If there were, let us say, a massive penal code for gun possession, what would happen? The only people giving up guns would be the lawful people. The bad people would keep their guns.

Ridding America of guns rests on the belief that the government

can do an effective removal; that the government can protect us from the bad guys once we are defenseless; that the government will not oppress us (Venezuela, Cuba, USSR, China, the Third Reich, Big Brother).

I would love to trust our government. The founding fathers did not. They believed an armed populace was the last protection against an oppressive government.

Let us remember Hitler said in 1935:

> *This year will go down in history. For the first time, a civilized nation has full gun registration. Our streets will be safer, our police more efficient, and the world will follow our lead into the future!*

But Thomas Jefferson opined:

--Laws that forbid the carrying of arms . . . disarm only those who are neither inclined nor determined to commit crimes . . . Such laws make things worse for the assaulted and better for the assailants; they serve rather to encourage than to prevent homicides, for an unarmed man may be attacked with greater confidence than an armed man.

--I prefer dangerous freedom over peaceful slavery.

--One loves to possess arms, though they hope never to have occasion for them.

--What country can preserve its liberties if its rulers are not warned from time to time that their people preserve the spirit of resistance? Let them take arms.

--The tree of liberty must be refreshed from time to time with the blood of patriots and tyrants. It is its natural manure.

--The course of history shows that as a government grows, liberty decreases.

--Let your gun be your constant companion on your walks.

--The constitutions of most of our States assert that all power is inherent in the people; that they may exercise it by themselves, in all cases to which they think themselves competent; or they may act by representatives, freely and equally chosen; that it is their right and duty to be at all times armed; that they are entitled to freedom of person, freedom of religion, freedom of property, and freedom of the press.

Hearing returns to normal

In the world of my 2022 Balboa Press *What if?* I imagined that we could not hear.

That we could not hear the birds, the TV, or the radio. That there was no music.

That closed-captioning was widespread because we could not hear anything spoken.

But in our normal world, closed-captioning is just an option. We can choose it if we want. We don't have to have it, because we can hear the spoken word. We can hear the birds. We can hear music. Life is good.

Intensity

On direct examination, we learn that Robert grows lilies, donates to the church, and is a good neighbor. On cross-examination, we learn that his lilies died, his church contributions were small, and that he threw his beer cans on the lawn.

Professor Wigmore (who to the law of evidence is what Joe Montana is to professional football) deemed cross-examination the greatest engine of truth known to mankind.

However, if sloth is one of the Seven Deadly Sins, what about its opposite, *intensity*?

One of my litigating husbands said about trying to please his wife, "I ran at it. I tried and tried. I bashed my head against the wall."

Bob Seger sang about his intensity as a performing artist:

> *out there in the spotlight*
> *you're a million miles away*
> *every ounce of energy*
> *you try to give away*
> *as the sweat pours out your body*
> *like the music that you play*
> --Gear Publishing Co./ASCAP

It is a metaphor for each of us bringing forth our best. The stressed and devoted parents, the cross-examining lawyers, the painters of large canvases, the painters of small ones.

> *say here I am,*
> *on the road again*
> *there I am*
> *up on a stage*

Each day the road goes on with a sameness--a dullness even--from which only intensity for tasks can rescue us. That intensity is our stage.

here I go again
playing the star again
there I go
turn the page

Interstate highways

Knoxville is the only place in the United States where a north-south interstate crosses an east-west interstate inside a city's limits.

The north-south interstate is I-75. The east-west interstate is I-40. The traffic problems are huge, as might be expected.

The problem is compounded by the fact that I-40 is a feeder for I-81, a heavily traveled north-south interstate. For a period, Knoxville was called "malfunction junction."

Now there are some partial ring roads that have slightly reduced the problem. But Knoxville's rush-hour TV and radio shows always lead with the traffic problems.

Irish brown soda bread

This is a lot of work. Soda bread takes longer to make than corn pone or grits, but it is worth the effort. There is no kneading, and no waiting for dough to rise.

1 and 3/4 cups all-purpose flour
3 and 1/2 cups stone ground whole-wheat flour
2 teaspoons baking powder
4 teaspoons baking soda
1 and 3/4 cups whole fat buttermilk at room temperature
3 tablespoons dark brown sugar
1/2 cup wheat term
1 and 1/2 cups natural bran
1 and 1/4 cups steel-cut oats
2 and 1/2 teaspoons sea salt

That is a lot of ingredients. You can see that it is healthy.

Spread a large cloth, maybe three feet by three feet, on your counter. This will catch the stuff you spill.

Make four batches of the dry ingredients in individual gallon plastic bags. Put three bags in the freezer for future loaves.

Put the contents of the fourth bag into your largest mixing bowl. (Just the dry ingredients.) If the brown sugar is lumpy, crush the lumps. Toss the dry ingredients until fully mixed.

Now add the buttermilk and mix it in until the whole mess is thoroughly wet and uniform. If you are doing this by hand, you will have to rotate the bowl as you work.

Preheat your oven to 400 degrees.

Butter two loaf pans (approximately nine or ten inches by five inches). Put parchment paper in the bottoms.

Divide the bread mixture between the two pans.

Bake in the middle of the oven until golden brown and crusty, about fifty minutes. Insert a slim wooden stick into each loaf to check for doneness. If the stick comes out clean, the mixture is baked through. If the stick is gunky, bake the loaves for another ten minutes. Check it again with the stick.

When the bread is baked through, unmold the loaves and cool them on a wire rack.

Enjoy with butter, marmalade, and a huge cup of hot cambric tea.

Leave-taking

The accomplishments of our children are farewells to us.

Oh, how proud we are of that child, outnumbered five-to-two, protecting the soccer goal against those odds. The five rush at him and his goalie again and again. He does not buckle, he gives his all. He shines with light.

But it is the light of leave-taking. He is telling us--and does not know he is telling us--"Goodbye, Dad. Goodbye, Mom. I'm on my own now. I can fight the fight. Thanks for your love."

Oh, how hard this is. He's our little boy. He does not need us to hover, shelter, protect any more. We have to back off, learn a new job description. Oh, how proud we are. Oh, how it hurts.

I stood in the driveway and cried when my oldest drove away, leaving for college.

It does not get easier from child to child. It is no easier with the second, no easier with the third.

Leave-taking means acceptance. We don't want it. We buckle, we rail. We don't want the change.

Leave-taking can have many forms. It can be rebellion, defiance, turf-definition. Sometimes it is as graceful as one child accepting responsibility for another. The older child brings your younger son off the rock face. The sun has set, it is growing cold, the lake is turning dark below. The older brings the younger down because we can't: "You stay here, Dad. Don't look. Don't worry. I'll get him. I love him, too."

Oh, how graceful, how simple, how fine--"You don't have a monopoly on love, Dad. I love him, too. Watch me. Farewell."

Oh, how it hurts. Farewell.

Living off the grid mentally

We live in chaos, keeping up with politics and news in the United States.

I have a friend, an excellent medical doctor and surgeon who listens to music when he is not working. Just music. No news, no politics. At work he does not talk about news or politics.

He and his wife eat out often. They do not talk about what is going on in the news or politics.

He lives a peaceful life. He chooses to do so. He probably does not vote. To cast an uninformed ballot would offend him.

His choice to live off the grid is understandable, admirable.

We who live surrounded by continual adversarial chatter suffer from our diet.

Lobster and scrambled eggs, improved

Equipment:
- bowl for mixing eggs
- large cast iron skillet with cast iron lid
- spray cleaner and paper towels for clean up

Ingredients:
- 2 live Maine lobsters, one and a quarter pounds or larger
- 12 eggs
- salt and pepper to taste

Directions:
- Break eggs into a bowl but do not scramble.
- Heat skillet on stove top until very hot.
- Have the lid ready in one hand.
- Throw lobsters into the skillet with your other hand, dump the eggs in fast, and get the lid on.
- When the thrashing stops, the dish is ready.

Loons

Loons talk of wildness, wilderness, loneliness, mourning, joy.

You are blessed to listen. All the airline tickets, all the bother in getting to Northwest Ontario are nothing. You have made it, once again, to moments of heaven.

Loons dive. They swim underwater using their wings. They carry their babies on their backs, and they talk, talk, talk.

They are heavy birds. On land, they can barely waddle, going ashore only to nest. When there is wind or a breeze, they head into it to get lift.

The loons talk to each other. They are not talking to you, but you are blessed to hear them.

Lust

Lust is a loose cannon, a massive, rolling, untied blackness. It crashes about, battering our psychic gunwales.

Poets often speak about lust. Wallace Stevens (1879-1955) describes Susanna and the leering elders:

> *Of a green evening, clear and warm*
> *She bathed in her still garden, while*
> *The red-eyed elders, watching, felt*
> *The basses of their being throb*
> *In witching chords, and their thin blood*
> *Pulse pizzicati of Hosanna.*

Hart Crane (1899-1932) was painfully candid:

> *Outspoken buttocks in pink beads*
> *Invite the necessary cloudy clinch of bandy eyes.*

Shakespeare's Hamlet, upset at his mother's hasty remarriage to Claudius, berates her:

> *Rebellious hell,*
> *If thou canst mutine in a matron's bones*
> *To flaming youth let virtue be as wax*
> *And melt in her own fire.*

So much for the poets. The only way to control lust is not to light the flame atop the candle. Avoid the circumstances of temptation. Do not go to the trendy fern bar where lovelies might palm your glutei. Go elsewhere. Don't put yourself in harm's way.

This might be called the potato chip rule: *"If you don't want to eat a bunch of potato chips, don't put them in your grocery cart."*

The potato chip rule is not courageous, but it is pragmatic. It would be more courageous to sally forth to the fern bar and test yourself. "Can I keep my mind on pure thoughts? Ah, but I really need to network. I need to advance my business. Am I not above carnal lust?"

Maybe. But what you are probably doing at the fern bar, if you are married, is making a down payment on court costs. Your bass will throb in witching chords (Wallace Stevens). It will sing to you of potato chips.

President Carter discussed lust candidly with *Playboy*'s interviewer. For that he was criticized, ridiculed, and viewed with alarm. He simply said that, yes, of course he had lusted after women from afar, mentally. Carter was aware of the impossibility of absolute thought control, the impossibility of Augustinian perfection, and he had the courage to say it openly.

For our children and grandchildren we can model a loving relationship. If we show them that we love our spouse, they will feel secure. They will model themselves on that.

Money returns

In the world of *What if?* I imagined that money was gone.

But with money alive and well, once more we have our customary greed, grasping, and capitalism.

Score is kept on the stock markets once more.

We can keep up with the Joneses, or--by golly!--we can beat the Joneses.

We have currency again. It is *"backed by the full faith and credit of the United States government."* That may comfort us, or not. We do not have to purchase gold to avoid using the paper currency, but we can buy gold if we want to do that.

Now that we have money, we return to neglecting our fellow man. We forget that our principal needs are food, shelter, clothing, and the affirmation of others.

Shipping resumes, because now its costs can be met.

Charitable giving falls off.

Church attendance declines. We don't need God, we think. Because now we have money instead.

Oxygen remains unchanged

In the world of *What if?* I imagined that the world's oxygen level of 21% was cut to 10.5%.

The result was immediately disastrous: All mammals and birds died. Worms, slugs, and snails survived.

But with oxygen at normal levels none of that happened.

Life went on, on our blessed earth, in our unique and God-given balance.

No one unable to walk

In the world of *What if?* I s imagined that people could not walk except with leg braces or walkers. That the lack of real exercise led to increased obesity and type two diabetes.

But in our normal world, we do walk, we exercise. And except for those who choose to be fat, diabetes does not increase.

On being unable to play the lute

I cannot play the lute.
My neighbor, he also
Cannot play the lute.
That is of no moment.
For, you see, the thing is,
It is I who will never know luteness.

Oh yes, I could, as you say,
Take lessons in lute.
I could remove this flaw.
But I won't.
It's because, it's because, well,
There are too many instruments now.
Time has marched on.

Pico della Mirandola had just one lute.
Now lutes are squared and cubed.
They're Braqued, Picassoed, and Einsteined.
Who can play them all?

Oh, once it was enough
To play the lute and ride the horse,
Write poetry,
Sing, throw some stones.
Life was simple,
All knowledge was in reach.
But not now.

Do you think I could just, well,
Get a little place somewhere
And maybe wind lute strings?
Something simple,
Something within my grasp,

Something, you know, finite?
I could put the strings
In little glassine bags.
Maybe I could do that.
Yeah, maybe that.

Ostriches

Milan Kundera's image for modern communication is six frantic ostriches, beaks opening and shutting feverishly, pressed up to the fence of their compound. Each tries to tell us how things are, how he ran up to the fence, what he had for lunch that day, how his feathers feel.

They do not listen to each other. Their messages are one-way. There is no exchange of ideas.

We do that sometimes:

"I feel so frustrated about my relationship with my boss."
"That's just like me; I . . ."
"My boss makes me do useless tasks, day after day."
"That's just like me; I . . ."

We might think that this form of agreement is a way to carry the other person's ideas a step further. Kundera says it is the exact opposite. All the "just like me" statements, he says,

> are a brute revolt against brute force,
> an attempt to free one's ear from bondage,
> a frontal attack the object of which is
> to occupy the enemy's ear. All man's life
> among man is nothing more than a battle for
> the ears of others.
> The Book of Laughter & Forgetting (1979)

We do not connect. No one asks the Grail Question: "Old man, why are you in pain?"

My beak is yellow. I see the mesh of the wire. My feathers are brown. Today for lunch I had cracked corn. Today I think I'll . . ."

Kundera left Czechoslovakia in 1975 for France, unable to publish in his native land. He knows censorship firsthand. As much as he hates political censorship, he hates and fears even more the isolation which cripples our minds. It is the censorship of "That's just like me; I . . ."

People die now

In the world of *What if?* I imagined that no one died. That we just lived on and--because of that--there was overpopulation and starvation.

But in the normal world, we age. We die at the end of our appointed rounds. We get killed by cancer, traffic accidents, or something else.

Doctors are needed.

Overpopulation is not a problem.

Pigeon Forge has pancake restaurants

In Pigeon Forge, Tennessee, you are never out of sight of a pancake restaurant, if you count waffles as pancakes with patterns.

There are that many pancake restaurants because people on vacation eat junk food. *"Hey, it's a vacation right?"* If people want pancakes, franchisers will build the stores. Capitalism will provide.

Americans are already obese and diabetic. *They are fat and diabetic by choice.* Pigeon Forge swells the numbers.

For children and adolescents aged 2-19 years in 2017-20201,
obesity affected 14.7 million children and adolescents.

Among 2- to 5-year-olds, obesity was 12.7%,
Among 6- to 11-year-olds, 20.7%, and among 12- to 19-year-olds, 22.2%.

Childhood obesity is also more common among certain populations. 26.2% among Hispanic children, 24.8% among non-Hispanic Black children, 16.6% among non-Hispanic White children, and 9.0% among non-Hispanic Asian children.

Obesity-related conditions include high blood pressure, high cholesterol, type 2 diabetes, breathing problems such as asthma and sleep apnea, and joint problems.

We are fat and diabetic by choice. It is not forced upon us. It is a decision.

Pigeon Forge: "Buy one pair of boots, get two pair free"

That's right. Who could refuse? This is marketing in Pigeon Forge, Tennessee. It must work, because the advertising has been running for over two years.

No one realizes--or cares?--that the price of the first pair includes the merchant's cost for pairs two and three.

P.T. Barnum did not say, *"A fool is born every minute,"* but he could have.

Pigeon Forge's Jurassic Park

In Pigeon Forge, Tennessee, there are a multitude of entertainments. One is the "Jurassic Park Boat Ride." In a boat, you travel a river. You meet mechanical dinosaurs. (The boat, while surrounded by shallow water, does not actually float; it is instead led by track.)

The ride is dark. Every few seconds a spotlight shines on a featured dinosaur which performs a movement. You hear sound effects until the scene goes dark again and you move on. There's an assortment of mannequins out front in pith helmets and khakis.

The ride is expensive. General admission for Jurassic Jungle Boat Ride in Pigeon Forge is $18.99 per adult, $13.99 for children ages 5-11, and $6.99 for children ages 3-4.

I had a young lady in my court who said that she was the ticket seller for the jungle boat ride. My daughter had recently done the ride with her children and had been displeased. So I asked the young lady what people said after finishing their rides. She said that the customers wanted their money back.

The Jurassic Park Boat Ride is still operating. This is because dinosaurs are a continual draw for children and because customers do not check online reviews.

Piss

Germans have a rich vocabulary of phrases, sayings, and individual words about defecation. *Scheisse* occurs in tens of usages. Defecation is even an aid to thinking. Martin Luther said his best ideas often came to him on the seat of ease.

English speakers on the other hand are rich in piss phrases, sayings, and individual words.

A *pismire,* also called a *pisamire,* is an archaic or dialect word for an ant, literally a urinating ant. It comes from the odor of formic acid characteristic of an ant hill. It is a word of Scandinavian origin.

A *pissant* is an insignificant person. We tell people to go away: *piss off!*

We waste something by *pissing it away.*

To urinate is to *take a piss.*

We say of someone, *"He's so poor he doesn't have a pot to piss in."*

"Don't *piss your pants."*

"Don't *piss into the wind."*

Planes and helicopters are here again

In the world of *What if?* I imagined that planes and helicopters were gone. That there was no heavier-than-air flight. That man turned to helium balloons. That air mail disappeared.

But now we once again have contrails in the sky. We travel by airplane. Commuter helicopters are common.

Prejudice

There is a wise story for your children and grandchildren. It imagines a place, the land of the sneetches, where "Star Belly" sneetches had bellies with stars, and the "Plain Belly" sneetches didn't.

This led to discrimination. The star-bellied ones were better. They knew it. What made them better was the star on their bellies.

Because they were better, they did not associate with the sneetches who had no stars. Those poor fellows were inferior. The sneetches with stars would not play ball with the ones lacking stars. They would not invite them to their frankfurter roasts. The ones with no stars had to sit in the back of the bus, eat at designated lunch counters, and drink from water fountains labeled for them.

In sneetch land there was no United States Supreme Court to fix invidious discrimination. But capitalism could do it in sneetch land: Sylvester McMonkey McBean could fix the discrimination.

He put stars on the bellies of those lacking stars, for a charge of three dollars per belly, using a machine. A sneetch merely entered one end of the machine's tube and--presto!--that sneetch came out the other end with a star on his belly.

All was now well.

Except all was not well, because the original Star Belly sneetches were distressed. This was wrong. They weren't better anymore.

Again, McBean had a capitalist's solution. For ten dollars per belly, he would take the stars off the sneetches who had been Star Bellies. The Star Bellies thought that was great, and they lined up to pay ten dollars, one after another. So once again, there was invidious discrimination.

Thereafter, it kept going. Back and forth. Every sneetch paid ten dollars to reverse his condition-of-the-moment, and the conversions continued until all their money was gone.

At that point, because there was no more money for him to make, McBean packed up and left, rich and happy.

Pride

When pride urges us to depart from the True Way, it whispers, "Yes, but what about . . ."

There is pride we unhesitatingly know is negative. The architect of the Thousand Year Reich, the playground bully, petty despots.

Psychiatrists call this negative pride "malignant narcissism." It is a blindness to all needs except one's own. These people treat the world as a pavilion for themselves. They must be the literal center of attention. They think of themselves as the ones to whom all external activity is dedicated.

It is said that Kaiser Wilhelm II--the man who took Germany into World War I--had such pride of self that he felt he deserved always to be the center of attention. His valet said that *at a christening, he wanted to be the baby; at a wedding, he wanted to be the bride; and at a funeral, he wanted to be the corpse.*

But the malignantly narcissistic are not always distant, removed in space or time. Judges see them every week. Sometimes the malignantly narcissistic are dominant, domineering, bossy--hands on hips and a sneer on the lips. Usually they are quieter and do their manipulation subtly. But always their family must dance to their tune, fill their needs, see things their way. Because after all, their way is the right way.

The malignantly narcissistic live in a lonely, grim hell--controlling others, shaping others' worlds, receiving no gratitude for their tremendously invasive misplaced labors.

Venomous self interest can come in small doses. If we bend others to our will, we deny those others their personhood and worth.

The truly proud have no flaws. The theologian Martin Buber said these people insist upon *"affirmation independent of all findings."* That is, "Don't confuse me with facts; reality is what I say it is."

But pride can be a virtue, the foundation of a positive self-concept. It is the motivating ethic in team spirit, in corporate teamwork, and in healthy patriotism.

Pride is essential to our children and grandchildren. We should encourage our little ones to feel satisfaction in a job well done.

If we know we are flawed, if we ask for help, then we are rooted in the real world. If we know ourselves, then we know we are not the spider to whom run all strands in the web. We will praise our children, our spouses, and ourselves in the confidence that a good day's work should be called just that. As Lennon and McCartney put it:

Hey, Jude,
You'll do.
Don't carry the world
Upon your shoulders.

Problem solvers

In O.Henry's *"Gift of the Magi,"* the newlyweds give each other their most prized possession--she, her hair (cut off and sold to buy him a watch chain); he, his watch (sold to buy combs for her hair).

Each had the problem of poverty and no Christmas gift to give. Each brought his/her best to the problem. That Christmas they gave gifts equal to the gifts brought to the baby Jesus.

It is a touching story. These two newlyweds are problem solvers. They had no gifts to give, and they figured out what to do.

Half of all marriages fail. But that is just a statistic for first marriages. Subsequent marriages fail at a much higher rate.

Is there an "O.Henry gift" for America's marriages? Not hair combs or a watch chain. Maybe it is the simple gift of giving.

We can give our time to a family with problems: We can listen. We can sacrifice our own agendas, our oh-so-important tasks.

We do not ask, *"What's in it for me?"* but rather, *"Can I help?"*

Reading is back

In the world of *What if?* I imagined that we could not read. That the stock markets used pictures of stocks where possible--of an apple for Apple stocks, or of a pillow for Microsoft.

That there was no print publishing. That the print publishers turned to audio versions.

But in our normal world, we read. Children learn to do it in school or they learn to do it with help from their parents.

Reflective listening

Parents and grandparents can use reflective listening to draw out a child in conversation. By paying close attention to what she is saying; commenting on it uncritically; and then asking questions.

The goal is understanding, not instruction. Not passing along data, or rules.

In families reflective listening happens in less than five percent of all conversation. Reflective listening says, *"What you say matters to me."*

The children of parents who listen reflectively develop confidence in their ability to perceive, to evaluate, and to express themselves. Because it is the child who leads the conversation, there is a cooperation which feels good to the child and to the parent.

Of course we must also _teach_ our children. When we teach, we lead the conversation. We say where the two of us are headed.

But in reflective listening, the child leads. In _teaching_, the child's thoughts are molded; in **reflective listening**, the child's thoughts are left intact.

It is tough to live where others make plans for you:

> *Suzanne, the plans they made*
> *put an end to you*
> *Sweet dreams and flying machines*
> *in pieces on the ground*
> *I woke up this morning*
> *and I wrote down this song*
> *just can't remember*
> *who to send it to*

Let us resolve that at least once each day we will let our children lead the discussion.

> *I've seen sunny days*
> *that I thought would never end*
> James Taylor, "Fire and Rain" (1970, Warner Bros. Records)

Religion is back

In the world of *What if?* I imagined that religion was gone.

But with religion again alive and well, there is once again a higher power. People again seek holy moments. Alcoholics Anonymous has a guiding star again.

Church attendance grows. *"In God we trust"* is restored to United States coins.

Theology schools are filled.

Karl Marx's "opiate of the masses" dictum is rejected for its foolishness, meanness, and supercilious sneering.

Life is good once more.

Samaritan

Things were slow at the office, so the lawyer decided to go to a continuing education seminar. When he got back, his partner asked him how the seminar had been.

"Not very useful. The guy told stories. Not much black letter law."

"Oh yeah? What kind of stories?"

"Well," the lawyer said to his partner, "one was about some Samaritan getting beaten up."

"Huh. Well, you've got a lot of messages to return."

"I got the Samaritan story when I just asked him a question. I just asked him who my neighbor was."

And so it is with lawyers. We make things complicated. Perhaps all of us do that.

The lawyer in Luke's gospel didn't want answers. He wanted to hear he was diligently questing. Two thousand and some years haven't changed us much.

One wise parent put it this way:

> *And you of tender years*
> *Can't know the fears*
> *That your elders grew by*
> *And so please help*
> *Them with your dreams*
> *They seek the truth*
> *Before they can die*
> Giving Room Music, BMI

This is Graham Nash's advice to children who see their parents picking through the morass of their adulthood, trying to do right, trying to leave nothing unattended.

All parents know that parenthood is keeping fourteen balloons in the air, touching them all, all the concerns, over and over, lest one fall to the ground and burst.

So Nash tells the children: Your parents have come a long way; give them some respite. All they need from you is your completeness, your simple acceptance.

The lawyer left the seminar before the teacher got to the part about children. He would have heard him say, "Of such is the kingdom of heaven."

Not very good black letter law. Not much good in court.

School shootings

What is the correct response? It is certainly not, *"Let's get rid of all guns."* That can't be done, except with a magic wand. But what then?

Attend every school board meeting. Attend every PTA meeting. Attend every public forum on education. Speak out against sloppy protection.

Put armed guards in the schools.

If your state doesn't yet have open-carry, lobby for it.

Have your open-carry parents walk through the schools. Randomly. When they can. When they are picking up their children.

Insist on a civilized environment for learning, the teaching of values. Accept no more lies from public officials that they are protecting our children.

> *Now the Chief Executive enters,*
> *and the press conference begins.*
> *First the President lies about the date*
> *the Appalachian Mountains rose.*
> *Then he lies about the population of Chicago,*
> *then the weight of the adult eagle,*
> *and the acreage of the Everglades.*
> --Robert Bly, 1970

Our lives are polluted, like the four creeks of our own Knoxville. Take a double handful of mud, gravel, and stones from the shore of First, Second, Third, or Fourth creeks, and what do you find? No life. Nothing.

Do the same thing in the Smokies, and you find nymphs, crawfish, caddis flies, striders.

We accept the death of our streams. Why not accept the death of our schools also?

What would happen with the next school shooting if four hundred parents walked off their jobs and went to that school. Sat in the classrooms, talking to the children about values, the importance of truth.

Would the school administrators see that we have had enough? Or will they keep taking their paychecks, business as usual, lying to us about the weight of the adult eagle, the acreage of the Everglades? Continue to tell us our streams are not dead, that they are just small waterways experiencing "transitional degradation pressures?"

School, 1949-1952

The boy threw up on the way to school,
Regularly,
A matter of course,
Compass-setting.
The stink of decomposing plankton
Would rise into his blowholes,
And make his bright eyes water,
Make the sidewalk swim.
His almost hairless body, half-formed,
Wet cetacean eyes casting about,
Sought protection, not ritual heaves,
Not emesis on neighborhood lawns.

His mother protected him when she could,
Let him swim in her shadow,
Helped him feed, hid him
When she herself was not in danger,
The denouncéd whore, the common slut,
The bright-eyed nurse.

He scraped his way along the sidewalks
Thinking six times nine, four times three,
Thinking bile-tinged thoughts.
He thought of the school cafeteria, steaming,
Waiting, windows fogged,
A place that sometimes had no food for whales.
He thought of home and crashing waves,
The leaping thrashing father,
Up, up into bright air,
Leaping high and falling back into the sea,
Killing what lay below him,
Denouncing the whore.

He wondered how it could be
That at home only she loved him,
Only his mother,
While at school many, many loved him.
Even the ladies in the cafeteria,
Even on the days
When there was no food for whales.

He thought of children, tiered and glowing,
Standing on stair steps reaching
All the way to heaven,
Reaching so high the air was thin and shimmering
Where the oldest stood, singing,
Singing in the school's foyer,
Singing Oh, little town,
Singing with no fear of megaliths
Falling, white-crusted, waves driven asunder,
Gulls sent screaming,
Their wingtips slapping foam.

He thought of his teacher who loved him,
Who loved his gray skin,
His smooth gray skin,
Who gave him stamps and stars.
At night, rising to breathe,
He saw her stars among the stars,
Her stamped cat shapes upon the constellations.
At night, rising to breathe,
He knew he wanted to live in school,
Wanted to breathe the dust of tempera paints
And construction paper forever,
Far from falling fear,
Far from barnacled screams.
He knew he wanted to live, and live, and live,
Without bile, without flukes,
Beyond the horizon, among the stars.

Seasons

We do not call up the seasons. They are beyond our control. They will continue without us.

> *God of the earthquake*
> *God of the storm*
> *God of the trumpet blast*
> *How does the creature cry woe*
> *How does the creature cry save*

As we age, we feel the seasons' change as a reliable contract. We rise and look out over the fields of ironweed and goldenrod, a splendor of purple and gold. East Tennessee ridges rise behind, and we know that surely winter will follow. Winter with browned and rattling stalks where radiance stands now, winter with joy, hugging our little people, the ritual cherishing of those we love.

> *God of the hungry*
> *God of the sick*
> *God of the prodigal*
> *How does the creature say care*
> *How does the creature say life*

Beyond winter's cold the air will sweeten. Green will poke through the brown leaves on the ground, the beginnings once more of ironweed and goldenrod.

We know that our children will have another and another rotation of seasons, that the contract will be fulfilled.

There will be time for all that is yet undone. There will be time for cherishing. There is no hurry.

God of the sparrow
God of the whale
God of the swirling stars
How does the creature say awe
How does the creature say praise

We watch our children grow with the ironweed, stronger each year. They feel the contract too.

They know there will be permanence beneath the changes, that their parents will be there to learn and laugh with them. They know that even after their parents are gone, there will still be the seasons, slow and majestic, carrying them and their own children.

God of the ages
God near at hand
God of the loving heart
How do your children say joy
How do your children say home
--1983, Jaroslav J. Vajda

Sloth

We have no preparation to be parents. No one in business would suggest running a company without preparation. *"So you want to be a CEO? Great! Here's a going concern. Good luck!"*

We parents commit obvious mistakes. We correct them slowly, or we over-correct. We make important decisions under stress. We have a shortage of role models, and in many instances the role models we have are poor ones.

Court systems are skilled in toting up the shortcomings of parents. Father ignored behavioral abnormalities. Mother did not consider that her son might have an ear infection, being wrapped up in her own problems.

How did these parents get that way? Was it sloth?

We know that _modeling_ behavior is fine, but _driving_ our children to be as organized as we are is not. Childhood should be a time of unhurried reflection and wonder. The children will have time enough later to become frazzled ninnies.

The more childlike wonder we can hold, the more peace for reflection we can carve out of the daily chaos, the better citizens we will be.

So we should organize our children's days for their peace, and we should claim peace ourselves by making it a shared goal.

Few of us fear sloth will catch us unawares. But medieval clerics thought sloth the deadliest of the seven deadly sins because of its threat to monastic life--laziness in the contemplation of God being a major failing in a monk.

I remember real sloths from my fifth-grade classroom films. They were the ERPI films--I don't remember what the acronym came from, but some of the films really were throw-uppable. There they were--it was 1952--in living black and white, hanging upside down, barely moving, contemplating like Oblomov where and whether to put that next foot.

For most of us non-monastic parents, sloth is not a sin to be taken seriously. But laziness is. Drifting is. Failing to plan ahead as mothers and fathers, failing to take the initiative--these restatements of sloth should get our attention.

It is a matter of balance: We can certainly over-plan. We should not be like the bus driver who stopped picking up passengers so that he could keep his bus on schedule. Our children need to be on the bus with us. The journey of life is too hectic and lonely without them.

Suffering

Come with me into those things that have
Felt this despair for so long--
those removed Chevrolet wheels that howl
With a terrible loneliness,
Lying on their backs in the cindery dirt,
Like men drunk, and naked,
Staggering down a hill at night
To drown at last in the pond.

Robert Bly (1926-2021), is not considered much of a poet. He did a lot of translations which are also poorly regarded. Still, I find this poem to be fine.

As to the lessening of human suffering, I wonder how well the legal profession does today. Many say that is not the task of the courts.

The people who say *it is not the task of the courts* are legal positivists. For them the only question is what does the letter of the law say? Once that is known, the law can be applied to a particular case. According to the positivists no more and no less should be done.

We know that law can be perverted to advance the well-being of only some of us. That was done in Germany from 1933 to 1945. It only took a redefining of "us' for the law to exclude Jews, dissidents, homosexuals, and the handicapped from the benefits of ordered society.

The positivists have a pure division of powers, a strict interpretation of the tripartite system of checks and balances. The problem of goodness or badness of a law--its effects--is a matter for the legislature.

It is correct that judges must not and cannot legislate. But any judge hearing family law cases, or criminal cases involving violence against the person, knows the sob of human despair.

Those judges know the words that tell of terrible loneliness, howling discouragement, thoughts of death.

What is a court system of positivists? Not much. Screw-turners, lever-pullers. A court with blinders on. A court system for 1933-45.

Tears in heaven

Eric Clapton's four-year-old son Conor fell from a 53rd floor window in New York. Clapton wrote "Tears in Heaven" with Will Jennings after a sustained period of grief.

This is an almost unimaginable loss. We might say poetically that we live in a valley and bad things can come into our valley. Each day might bring happiness or its opposite. There is the Christian comfort of life after death.

> *Would you know my name*
> *if I saw you in heaven?*
> *Would you hold my hand*
> *if I saw you in Heaven?*
> *Would you help me stand*
> *if I saw you in heaven?*
> *Would you be the same*
> *if I saw you in heaven?*
> --Drumlin Ltd./PRS

Teleporting by coordinates is no more

In the world of *What if?* I imagined that we could teleport to a location if we knew its full description in coordinates, e.g., *35.9606384 degrees north and 83.9207392 degrees west* for Knoxville.

I postulated that in such circumstances, adultery became easier because one could come and go without being seen.

There was no need for airlines with such teleportation.

But in our normal world, we fly in airplanes or drive in cars, and we are discreet in our personal behavior.

Teleporting by sight is gone

In the world of *What if?* I imagined that if we could see it, we could go there immediately by teleportation.

And regrettably some people made the mistake of going to the moon without space suits.

But, with this form of teleporting gone, children's soccer games are now played normally.

Hiking in the Smokies returns to what it was before: walking.

The Christmas Ham

Barbara Robinson published *The Best Christmas Pageant Ever* in 1972. It is the story of the Herdmann family, poor with little to share. And yet they do share. They have the spirit of Christmas.

Many people sneer at sharing. They tell Jean Anouilh's Becket not to give money to the poor: "*The poor are cold. What they need is blankets. They will just use the money to buy drink.*" And Becket answers, "That too will warm them."

The Herdmann children are desperately poor. They are unwashed, the project kids who got roped into a Christmas pageant by mistake. But they heard _homeless, left out, cold-shouldered_. They heard putting the baby in a motel drawer instead of a bed of its own. They heard that Baby Jesus was getting a lousy start in life.

And they cried. Tough, mean Imogene Herdmann cried. And so the Herdmann children brought the best gift that they had, all that they had, their Christmas ham.

"Hey! Unto you a child is born! He's in there, he's in the stable! Go and see, go on!" yells angel Gladys Herdmann. "There's a baby in there, people, and he's just like us Herdmanns!"

> *I look out at the white sleet falling as we left Connecticut,*
> *And the winter leaves swirled in the wet air after cars*
> *Like hands suddenly turned over in a conversation.*

These are lines from Robert Bly's "Sleet Storm on the Merritt Parkway" (1962).

> *I think of the many comfortable homes stretching for miles,*
> *Two and three stories, solid, with polished floors,*
> *With white curtains in the upstairs bedrooms,*

And small perfume flagons of black glass on the window sills,
And warm bathrooms with guest towels, and electric lights . . .
What a magnificent place for a child to grow up!

The Herdmanns did not get polished floors, guest towels, or warm bathrooms. They and Baby Jesus got hand-me-downs and bureau drawers to sleep in. So the Herdmann children bring Baby Jesus the best they have, because they know poverty.

Can we avoid apartness when Christmas comes around this year? Are we pure enough to give away our Christmas ham?

The undemanding child

Do you have a child who is grateful for whatever comes? For whatever you give her? A child who will be delighted even with a crumpled Kleenex? Because you have given it to him?

These children are special. If you have one of the grateful children, you are privileged. You have a window on biblical peace. You can indeed sit at the feet of that child and learn.

For such is the kingdom of heaven. Christ told the apostles that they were to let the children come to him out of the crowds, forbid them not- -those unnecessary, trivial distractions to the teaching rabbi.

For Jesus knew that children break through adult accretions of inattention, and free us to see the beauty of this moment, these people, these rocks, these flowers.

But the gospel phrase, *for such is the Kingdom of Heaven,* only hints at what we can learn from an undemanding child. He sees the world without preconception, without suspicion, fear, or agenda.

She sees today's events now, and she is fascinated with them. She sees the present as the only thing to which she should give her attention.

"That ain't much," we might say. and in one sense that is true. If we adults saw only the present and its hues, there would be little planning. We might get swamped in sitting and looking.

But, have we ever known the undemanding child to be lethargic? No. He has more life force than any skeptical child, than any skeptical adult.

The point is that we can learn from this child. If such is the kingdom of heaven, she allows us to see the complexity of the folds of the Kleenex, the angles, the shadows, the caves in the tissue.

There is an American Indian myth about the black crow of death. It teaches that this sequential continuity we experience, this succession of days, should be lived as though the crow of death were always perched on our left shoulder, just where we could see it if we looked quickly enough. And knowing this, we are to live with wisdom, with maturity based on ultimate and lasting values--such as kindness and wonder--not on competition, advantage or fear.

Maybe instead of whimsical yard flamingos--or perhaps in addition to them--we could have large black plastic crows of death. *Memento mori.*

This undemanding child is not a rarity. She exists in every child. Fascinated by smooth rocks, by thistles, by breezes off the hillsides.

Suffer such thoughts to come unto me and forbid them not.

TVA dams stay with us

In the world of *What if?* I imagined that all the TVA dams simply vanished.]

And that as a result there was massive flooding.

I imagined that there was no river shipping on the 652 miles of Tennessee River from Knoxville to Paducah, Kentucky.

And that the boating and tourism associated with flat water were gone.

But in our normal world, we have the dams. All is well. Tourism and flat-water boating flourish. Children learn to water ski. Boat docks sell boats and gas. And the boat docks rent out slips as usual.

Westminster Kennel Club 2023

Year upon year, a pageant of dogs. There was a new breed in the show this year. And there was again the usual patter about "family friendly," "charming personality," "boisterous."

There is a mockumentary film called *"Best in Show."* It was done in the year 2000 by Christopher Guest and Eugene Levy. If you haven't seen it, watch it as soon as you can.

But all the 2023 patter and time-worn phrases remind me of my own parody written years ago:

The German Blue Tick Picker has a long and difficult ancestry.

Indeed from earliest times it has had few friends.

Self-possessed, it will not hunt, herd, or retrieve, steadfastly resisting all efforts at utility.

The German Blue exists today solely because of his striking devotion to procreation.

Not friendly to children, the Tick Picker requires a great deal of open space for its rambunctious nature.

With a matted and twisted coat, this is a dog which requires daily grooming.

The Blue gets along best with a servile master.

Despite its name, the German Blue Tick Picker is not picky about food, and will eat almost anything.

The German Blue Tick Picker, number 8.

William Kirksey Swann

This rather longish name is the birth name of my Georgia grandfather. He later changed his name, only using "Kirk" for his middle name. Today, you would have to go to a Chancery Court to do a name change. But he just did it, and that was that.

I took the "Kirksey" and used it for two of my books, *Kirksey* (Balboa Press, 2021) and *More Kirksey* (Balboa Press, 2021).

My grandfather played dominoes in the stable beneath the courthouse in Covington. While he did that I would climb the courthouse stairs to the bell tower and watch the works run. After a while, I would go back to my grandfather and watch him in the dominoes games. When the games were over, we would walk home.

Although my grandfather had no legal training, once a week he held a court dealing with local matters. Today we would call it a municipal court. I was there in his court on a day when white boys had been picked up by the police for throwing watermelons at black houses. My grandfather scolded the boys and told them not to do it ever again. I imagine that their parents did more than just scold them.

My father stayed with his father's "Kirk" as well, becoming William Kirk Swann Jr. My father was a thoracic surgeon. I have written some pieces about him in this book using a moniker, WKSMD.

I was christened William Kirk Swann III. Because I figured three was enough, there is no William Kirk Swann IV.

My sons are Christopher Danforth Swann and Ian Kirk Swann. So at least the "Kirk" lives on with Ian. And Christopher named one of his three sons Alexander Kirkman Swann. So "Kirk" lives on there as well.

WKSMD and the proctologist

My father was a great diagnostician, as well as an excellent thoracic surgeon.

He diagnosed himself with hemorrhoids. That's what this vignette is about, the diagnostician.

The scene: diagnostician face down on the examining table, pants off. Proctologist approaches, spreads the buttocks, laughs. Says, *"Hell, Doc, you've got a tick on your ass!"*

WKSMD shaving in China

My father served in China during World War II. He got there by troop ship from our east coast to India, where he flew "over the hump" into China.

It turned out that China was the front in the war which never opened, so my father never went into combat.

Before volunteering for the Army, my father had been intending to practice obstetrics and gynecology. However, in China he became interested in chest surgery, which became his field when he returned to the United States after the war. One of his patients in China had been mauled by a tiger.

Every hot day in China my father shaved in the shelter of the orderlies' tent. The Chinese orderlies would gather around and watch and talk.

My father had lots of chest and leg hair. The Chinese are essentially devoid of body hair. As the Chinese discussed what they were watching, my father repeatedly heard one word.

After several days my father asked his translator what the word meant. The translator told him that the word meant *"monkey."*

WKSMD: If I had known . . .

My father smoked in World War Two. Lucky Strikes. The cigarettes were free. At times he was short of breath.

He died at age 77, October 8, 1990, undergoing an abdominal aortic aneurysm resection. It was not expected. He had chosen to have the surgery. He had chosen his surgeon.

His autopsy revealed moderately severe emphysema, severe calcific coronary atherosclerosis, fibrosis in the ventricular septum suggesting previous ischemic injury, and hypertrophy of both ventricles.

At one point in the 1980s he said to me, *"Hell, Bill, if I had known I was going to live this long, I would have taken better care of myself."*

Printed in the United States
by Baker & Taylor Publisher Services